To beautiful
Satya
from
Melissa & Riley

Monty's
Marvelous
Adventures

Written by
Dori Edwards

Illustrations by
Ryan Carr

Thank you to our friends at Montecito Bank & Trust
for helping to make Monty's book possible.

First edition printed December 2020.

Written by Dori Edwards
Illustrations by Ryan Carr
Layout design by Deanna Buley

ISBN 978-0-9841678-3-8

Published by Santa Barbara Zoo
www.sbzoo.org

Introduction

On March 17, 2020, the Santa Barbara Zoo closed to the public due to a global pandemic. Three days later, a little penguin named Monty started to make a big difference.

A hand-raised Humboldt penguin, this curious bird enjoyed exploring with his keepers and although the Zoo was empty of guests, it was filled with the adventures of a now-famous penguin—Monty! He explored the Zoo, meeting HoneyBun the rabbit, Bangori the gorilla, Michael the giraffe, and the tortoises, always making sure to find a favorite leaf along the way.

Monty's adventures were shared online and with each new video, Monty brought more and more joy. People of all ages and from all around the world proclaimed their affection for the little bird that brought smiles to their day.

During uncertain times, Monty brought certainty that good exists. As people were quarantined in their homes and disconnected from one another, Monty connected everyone through their shared love of his love for the world around him.

When the world felt a little lost, Monty helped it find its heart! He taught people to accept differences. He reminded people that life is in the little things and with each hug he gave his keeper Ellie, people remembered that love is the most important thing.

There once was a penguin named Monty
A curious little creature
His steps were light and jaunty
And he lived for adventure.

Monty wasn't like the others
He had scars upon his back
But no one is like another
And that's the truest fact.

It matters not what you wear
And it's okay if you feel scared
What matters is you're aware
Of the open heart you bare.

Feeling brave in his tuxedo
Monty was ready to go
He hopped on to land
And waddled down the road.

He walked into the jungle
And then into the woods
He walked as far as he could
Into other animals' neighborhoods.

The first creature he saw
Had some giant, furry hands
With a square-y, scary jaw
He was larger than a man!

This thing wasn't a penguin
He didn't have a beak
He had no pair of wings
But on his back a silver streak.

Monty felt alarmed
By this creature's obvious strength
He thought, Why don't I have arms?
Or a pair of fangs?

"My name is Bangori
I am a great ape
There's a pretty good story
Of why I am this shape.

Though I may seem stern
Or like I wear a frown
It's important that we learn
Why a smile turns down.

See, I have a thick brow
To protect my smart mind
It may look like a scowl
But it's just how I'm designed.

Behind this serious look
I can be quite kind
Just like any book
It matters what's inside.

My body is full of might
To help me through forestland
Your body is small and light
To ride waves to the sand.

My arms help me climb trees
Your flippers work in the sea
Though I'm larger on the outside
You're just as strong as me.

We may differ in our size
As everyone can see
But for how we spend our time
It's who we're meant to be."

So Monty said goodbye
And waddled on his way
Wondering what more he'd find
On this funny, sunny day.

As Monty walked about
What he saw gave him a shock
Some legs were sticking out
From underneath a rock.

He wondered why this creature
Carried a shell on its back
Why have this funky feature?
This odd, mobile shack.

It must make him slow
And he wouldn't win a race
Then out from down below
The tortoise poked his face.

"I may not be swift
No need to be in haste
I stop and enjoy the gifts
Of this beautiful place.

What your speed does for you
My shell does for me too
They're there just in case
We ever feel unsafe.

Your feathers keep you dry
While out in the ocean
My shell protects my spine
When sleeping or in motion.

Things might take me a while
I have a different pace
But it's just a different style
Of getting to the same place."

When Monty turned around
He couldn't believe his eyes
Up way off the ground
Was an incredibly tall surprise!

As big as a two-story house
A giraffe looked straight down
At this tuxedo-wearing mouse
Baffled by what he'd just found.

Monty's mind was full of thoughts
Like, Why was his neck so long?
Why was his skin covered in spots?
Why am I not that tall?
Why can't I be? Why not?

The giraffe looked at Monty
To the curious bird he said,
"I have the answers you seek
For the questions in your head.

You see I can reach the trees
And eat all that I wish
Your shape helps with your speed
So you catch a lot of fish.

So different in our colors
Both protect us from others
My pattern helps me camouflage
From a hungry lion entourage.

And from the ocean below
The white on your front
Looks only like the sun's glow
To a seal on the hunt.

Four legs and lots of height
Or short and on two feet
Both ways are just right
They help us live and eat.

We have different faces
And look at different views
We may live in different places
But I'm really just like you.

We both have eyes that see
Two ears that help us hear
We both have hearts that beat
For our families far and near."

Monty learned so much
Like not to be in a rush
To take the time to learn
And give everyone a turn.

If you're willing to explore
Even when you're afraid
There are wonders galore
When you're curious about each day.

Having spots on your skin
Is so very unique
Like the dimple on your chin
Or the freckles on your cheek.

Monty learned that things are full of love
No matter what their size
He learned that no one is above
And to love all is to be wise.

With flippers, fins, or hands
It is not what we see
But that we understand
We're all meant to be.

Monty looked at his best friend Ellie
His keeper at the Zoo
A human and a penguin
As different as me and you.

They didn't look alike
They couldn't even talk
But she was very kind
And took him on lots of walks.

She helped him to be brave
And he made her smile
She loved the hugs he gave
How they laughed all the while.

All that Monty knew
Was together they had fun
When looking you see two
But through love they are one.

Their differences didn't matter
This zookeeper and bird
And Monty wanted to show her
What he couldn't say with words.

So he looked and saw a flower
Fallen beneath his feet
He gave it to this friend
So different than he

He thought,
We're all different shapes
And no one should feel shame
Because underneath the surface
We're all just the same

And all creatures become gentle
When in love they are showered
So, thanks for being my friend
Here's a pretty flower.

About Monty

When Monty was just a teeny, tiny little penguin chick he was adopted by his foster feeder family, Montecito Bank & Trust, or MB&T as the locals from Santa Barbara call them. MB&T is the largest community bank on the Central Coast and has been serving the Santa Barbara community since 1975—that's a long time ago! They are known for being generous with their community support which is why they jumped at the chance to sponsor Monty. Their friends at the Santa Barbara Zoo asked for donations to help make sure that Monty had all the food and fun that he would need for the rest of his life.

Wondering how Monty got his name? MB&T had a special contest and let all of their employees vote! And they chose Monty which comes from the word Montecito. And you might also recognize the Cito part as the name of Monty's son.

Monty and his son, Cito, have become MB&T's mascots. MB&T employees go out into the community and teach local students about being responsible and smart with their money. MB&T uses "Monty the Saver" and "Cito the Spender" to teach kids about spending and saving using very fun lessons. Kids love learning lessons with Monty and Cito!

As part of the MB&T family, Monty and Cito receive fun gifts from MB&T on their birthdays like fish "cakes" or fish themed birthday parties, and they get special visits from MB&T employees throughout the year. MB&T employees always knew that Monty's playful spirit was destined for greatness, but they could have never imagined that he would become a penguin celebrity that brings smiles to so many people around the world with his marvelous adventures!